T0105545

TRAVELING STREAMS

A Reflective Journey

Lynn M. Dixon

Order this book online at www.trafford.com
or email orders@trafford.com

Most Trafford titles are also available at major online book retailers.

Printed in the United States of America.

ISBN: 978-1-4269-4207-5 (sc)
ISBN: 978-1-4269-4208-2 (e)

*Our mission is to efficiently provide the world's finest, most comprehensive book publishing
service, enabling every author to experience success. To find out how to publish your book,
your way, and have it available worldwide, visit us online at www.trafford.com*

Trafford rev. 08/27/2010

 www.trafford.com

North America & international
toll-free: 1 888 232 4444 (USA & Canada)
phone: 250 383 6864 ✦ fax: 812 355 4082

Dedication

*To all of those wanderers and travelers who seek to find the truth
and beauty in the people in all spaces and places.*

Lynn M. Dixon

*"Though we travel the world over to find the beautiful, we must
carry it with us or we will not find it."*

Ralph Waldo Emerson

Midwestern Writings

Upon returning from Paris, France
On April 2, 1996

April 6, 1996

Dear Kay,

I hope that you received my postcard; actually I sent you two but I think that I forgot to put the address on the first one. I was sitting outside the Louvre and had a few distractions. One man, who was selling something, saw that I was trying to concentrate, but wanted to know if I was an American.

I took my retirement money from the University system, hard years of blood and sweat for working at Chicago State, Prairie State and South Suburban. My travel agent got me a United Vacation packet for only $969 which included airfare and hotel with a continental breakfast. She asked if I was sure that I wanted to do this alone and I said a resounding, "Yes." At that point, I could not think of anything worse than Chi-Town in my life!

Anyway, I did it! I am so proud of myself and I was the first in my generation in the family to go "abroad." Ma had been to Germany and Morocco years before to visit a cousin. So, I went on March 26th of this year. Their time is seven, now eight hours ahead of ours. The time changed on Palm Sunday while I was there. Interestingly enough, I flew over with a young woman named Anne from the Seattle area.

It was her first time too and we were really excited on the plane. I fidgeted for quite a while as she read *Waiting to Exhale* by Terry McMillan and she was not a woman of color. She was cool and it seems that as you

1

cross over the Atlantic, they want to sedate you so you can chill. Every time, we looked up, the flight attendants were bringing us more free wine or some type of drinks. It was as if they were saying, "Cool out and go to sleep." And, we did.

Oh, Kay, there is so much to tell so I could never write it all. The first thing I found out is that none of my French worked so I was discouraged and afraid to use it. I just learned not to ask the French anything. The people who saved me were the hotel staff who was bilingual and the Office of Tourism which was in walking distance. They helped the tourists for free. They helped me figure out the bus schedules or trains or whatever mode of transportation I chose. I stuck with the bus line and spent six nights in Paris.

I went out immediately to get my feet wet and came back shortly feeling somewhat defeated. I spent 50 francs for some chicken wings at McDonalds because they could not understand what I was saying when I said, "How much?" (In French) They stood and looked at me like I was from another planet. If you can't communicate, they will cheat you. So I learned to count, point and the whole bout. Paris is extremely expensive and I went with only $200 to spend. Everybody kept telling me how much nerve I had. With what I had been through here, I felt that I had nothing to lose. I made it back to Chicago with enough money to get a shuttle back to Ma's in Hyde Park.

So, I'll give you the highlights. I took a Paris Vision Tour, on a bus, and saw the many landmarks. (You plugged in headphones and chose your language to listen to the tour guide. You could choose from 14 languages). I saw the Seine River, the Louvre, Avenue Champs Elysees with the Arc de Triomphe sitting over it; Notre Dame Cathedral; The Ritz; Cartier's; Garden of Luxembourg; Hotel des Invalides; the Bastille and the Eiffel Tower which is gigantic.

This young woman sat next to me and when she said, "Excuse me." I said," You speak English!" We both were so excited and we never stopped talking. She had been there longer and knew more and explained how to survive as an American. She was from Indiana. She was traveling with two other women and they seemed surprised to see how easily we clicked. She was leaving Paris the next day and reminded me to just point for the things I wanted when all else failed. Her name was Marsha Lynn. She had my name!

Everyday that I ventured out, I got lost; but, I was determined so I always found my way. The next day, I caught a bus and went back to the

Louvre. I enjoyed the walk in the Garden of Tulileries across the street from the Louvre. I was listening to one of my minister's tapes and there was a light mist. As he spoke of doves, some white birds flew close by. I felt that it was a mystical experience.

A Frenchmen took my picture and wanted 150 francs. I told him that I only had 27. He took it and smoothed down my hair with his hands. He asked if I was an American and seemed to be intrigued. Right after I got the picture, I saw two black women from California traveling together. They were from San Francisco and the Oakland area.

Later, I went into the Louvre. It cost 45 francs and I really was not in the mood. I feel you really need someone with you or a specific reason for taking the tour. When I saw all of the school groups, somehow a red flag went up and I just got some brochures. One is enclosed; plus it would take days to see it all but at least I can say that I was there.

But Kay, here's the deep part. It was on the first postcard. As I was waiting for my bus which did not come, the rain started. I felt like crying so I started walking. I saw all of these policemen. I looked and there was an employee protest going on. They marched in a large group huddled very tightly together and had a big protest sign. The streets were blocked off and that was why the bus was delayed. It was so exciting. I thought, "So, the whole world is in trouble. It is universal." Don't you just love it? They were the staff from the Louvre marching over some unhappy cause! Finally, my bus came after they re-opened the streets and I boarded my bus and headed back to the hotel.

Everything in Paris is so small and tiny. The cars are petite, the baths and so are the rues or streets. Fat people must have an awful time in the baths, showers and even beds. As I think about it, I do not recall seeing any fat people, while there. Anyway, this letter would never end, Kay, if I told you all of it. Saturday, I stayed in my room and worked on my manuscript. When I called my mother, she said, "Lynn, write!" That was my major goal for going, other than to heal my mind, body and soul.

But the highlight of the trip to me was going to the Sacre-Coeur in Montmartre- a church that sits high up on a hill. From the top, you can stand and look out over all of Paris. On the way, I was walking after getting directions from the hotel receptionist. Of course, I got lost. I saw a man peeing on the street and knew I was lost. But what really let me know that I was in harm's way was when I came upon some buildings that looked like the projects in Chicago. These buildings had graffiti on the outside and I felt quite vulnerable. After saying a prayer, I saw a very handsome blond man putting gas in a big luxury tour bus. I showed him the piece of paper with the name Sacre Coeur written on it that the woman from the hotel had given to me. He said, "Hi! I am on my way there to pick up a group." HE SPOKE ENGLISH! He told me to hop in and we talked the whole time. He took me there and said he was from Holland.

He told me that there were 240 steps to climb or I could pay 7 francs for the elevator to ride up to the church. I got out and thanked him. I enjoyed the climb. There were so many people all around. It was more like a bazaar. The older people were probably inside praying for their souls and the younger people were hanging out. Many people were selling their wares, holding them up and trying to get your attention. The brothas had their stuff laid down on the ground and dared you to step on it. Sound familiar? Smile. It is the same all of the over world.

Anyway, back to the service. I had called beforehand and knew what time the English speaking service would be held. It was the Palm Sunday service and it was absolutely beautiful. The church had stained glass windows and a huge picture of Christ that made it look like he was coming towards you. There were a lot of sections that had several candles burning as well. The speakers looked as though they were college-aged and they did the service in English, French, Spanish and Dutch to name a few. One person could switch over and do all the languages as he or she read the text. Just amazing and we can barely speak English!

Afterwards, we took sacraments and I was fortunate enough to get mine from the High Priest in the most decorated robe. I felt tears welling up as I realized how greatly God had blessed me after all of my dilemmas. Later, after descending the stairs and the street, itself, I found my way back to the hotel easily. On the way back, I stopped by a McDonald's and met a couple from Chicago. Ole Mickey D's saved my life. It was all I could afford and once I even found a grocery store to put some ham, bread and salad dressing in my room. I had a small refrigerator in my room and I also had a small balcony.

On the last day in Paris, I took a bus to the Sorbonne University. It was so beautiful with marble floors, mahogany wood and a lot of glass, like glass doors. I walked in the foyer and I can at least say that I have entered its doors. I saw students studying and I even ate, yes, at Mickey D's, which was filled with students. Of course, I got lost on the way, but again, not on the way back. When I got back to my room, I again worked on my manuscript.

I will close for now Kay. On the flight back to the States, we took the new 777 Boeing back. It was its maiden flight and everyone was excited. It was huge. When the pilot stood down by the wing, he looked like a midget. On the way back, I met a music teacher from Harvard. We talked so much and she said that she had never crossed the ocean so quickly. I also saw two movies, *Sabrina* and *The American President*. We landed in Washington D.C, and I had to change planes for a flight to Chicago. On the way, the flight was direct, because God knew I needed an immediate reprieve. I will close for now but at least you can see that Paris got my creative juices flowing and now for the bestseller!

Love,
Lynn

4/1996
Chicago, IL

My Spiritual Friend: A True Story

"Hello, Mary! This is Nita. Call me honey!" This is the first time I heard this voice on my answering machine, after moving in my new apartment with a new phone number in Chicago Heights. The voice was quivering and sounded like that of a female senior who probably lived alone. The first spiritual thing is that she called me Mary. That is the name of my aunt for whom I was legally responsible. She presently lives in a nursing home. The next thing that truly caught my attention is that her name was Nita. That is the name of my closest first cousin.

Little did I know that these messages would continue for over fourteen months. On a couple of occasions, I picked up and told this friend, that she had the wrong number, but the calls kept coming in to me. Well, my life grew progressively more challenging as I embarked on a new job. I came to appreciate these messages of concern from my friend, Nita.

On some days, I would walk in from work. I would see the light blinking. I would push the button before sitting down and the voice would say, "I'm so worried about you, I don't know what to do. Please call me, honey."

Another time, she called in a rather desperate tone saying, "Call Nita. Please call, Nita." Of course, I did not have her number but took the message as a sign and called my own cousin, Nita. I told my cousin about my mystical friend and what led me to call her. She responded, "That is wild! I am so glad you followed through because I really need to talk."

Anyway, these calls averaged about two or three times a week. Once, I decided that Nita and I needed to have a reality check. I picked up while she was still on the line and reminded her that she had the wrong number. She said weakly, "Please hang up so I can leave a message." I did. She seemed so fragile and it was a delicate matter. I understood and vowed to not try that again.

This led me to believe that her friend Mary was either someone from her past or she was remembering a portion of her life when times were more bearable. I had witnessed my own Aunt Mary Lou choose what she wanted to remember and disown the more bitter experiences.

On another occasion, I came in from work, frustrated and extremely agitated and ready to quit. I saw the blinking light on the answering machine, pushed the button and Nita started talking. She talked longer than she had ever talked. She talked about Mary's cute baby and how she should take care of herself. She talked about their shopping spree and how much she enjoyed it. It went on and on as a happy narrative.

As I listened to her joy and chatter, I realized that it was like listening to a soft ballad. Before I knew it, I had begun to undress and take off my work clothes and my brow began to smooth as I started moving around the apartment and forgetting the crap from work.

Nita was my elder. She became my guardian angel for the rest of the time that I spent in that apartment. At times, I felt so alone and her voice was there letting me know that there were other lonely friends out there.

Once, I told one of my sisters about Nita's calls and she said, "That's deep!" Right before our journey together ended, I was trying to decide whether I should leave that apartment and step out on faith. I came in from work and saw the blinking light and pushed the button. She said," Honey, I called to say good-bye. My son's coming to get me. I am moving to Florida. Bye, sweetie. I love you."

This was the last time I heard my spiritual friend's voice. After hearing that message, I knew that it was time for me to move on. I did. Life is beautiful. There's always a friend out there at the bottom of the well. She gave me encouragement and I gave her a listening ear!

7/1996
Evansville, IN

Reflections

You can't protect a man's reputation,
No money, no intimidation,
Nothing- absolutely nothing can shield a
Man from what others will say
Of his actions and morality.

February 6, 1998
Chicago, IL

27 Chicago Vignettes

Window Washer Bravado   #1

Yesterday while working on Michigan Avenue, I looked out of my window because I saw this rope- hanging from the building. Later, I noticed that it was actually a pulley! Then, I saw that it was a man sitting on a small board cleaning the windows of the building, one pane at a time!

I looked closer and noted the precision with which he worked. He looked like he could have been in his 30's. I felt," That is so brave to take on job like that!" And here we are, afraid to do the small things in life. This man puts his life on the line every day! It taught me a lesson. Forge ahead with courage. It could always be worse. Hats off to the window washers of the skyscrapers!

1/15/2000

Chicago's Bus Drivers #2

When I got off from work from a new temporary assignment, I had to try a new bus route to get home. The first female bus driver was extremely kind and at peace with herself. I then transferred to the second bus. I somehow felt very welcome.

Everybody seemed so warm and cozy and comfortable. As I stumbled on in my own inner upheaval, a gentleman rose, smiled and gave me his seat. He seemed honored to do so. I gladly accepted and was seated. Years ago, I would have felt that taking CTA would have been a put-down, but now in my wiser, stress- free seeking days, I see taking the bus as a huge blessing.

No cursing the other drivers as I drive; looking for parking, nor wondering if the mechanics of the car will continue to work. I have experienced bus drivers who have the patience of Job, offering kindness and sensitivity to everyone who boards and there are several appreciative riders. Hats off to the CTA drivers!

1/15/200

LaSalle Street Church   #3

Today, I went to LaSalle Street Church. It was the second Sunday I had gone in a row. They're doing a three-part series on *Financial Stewardship*. Last week's sermon was focused on generosity and giving even when you're poor. It helped me tremendously. I went on to support my sister, stayed with my mother and received a temp assignment on Michigan Avenue in a room alone and with a window. Yeah.

Today, the sermon was on *Claiming Debts* and a tribute to the legacy of Dr. King. The children were adorable, singing, "Jesus Loves Me." The songs, the message and the pianist were all so comforting. It was interesting to see other cultures striving to understand the feelings of the discriminated or the oppressed. Hats off to those who attempt to try and understand. Without those types, we wouldn't be as far as we are!

1/16/2000

Good News #4

The first cultural event I attended was at the Chicago Historical Society. I went with Ma and the other seniors from the Hyde Park Neighborhood Club. There was so much nostalgia there. First when we went to the club, I recall playing there with the Hyde Park Band. We saw then, Senator Thompson and played for him. (He later became the governor of Illinois.)

Later, in the early 90's we went there to the Hyde Park Neighborhood Club, to see the Rev. Barbara King of Atlanta. Ma and I went to see her speak as a guest of a Chicago church. Anyway, Ma, me and about 20 seniors boarded a school bus. The seats were so small and tight. I also remembered that I had driven one of these big buses and remembered what a brave feat that had been. All those lives in my hands, but at the time, I thought nothing about it. I needed the money and all the kids were safe with me.

Anyway, after all that digressing, back to the sunny Friday of January 7th of 2000. The seniors were just as snug and dependent as the small children that I had once driven. We arrived at the Chicago Historical Society (now the Chicago History Museum) to see the exhibits called *Good News* and *Wade in the Water*. One honored the life of Thomas Dorsey and other Chicago gospel writers.

The other exhibits focused on a variety of black musical geniuses. It was interesting to see the seniors move through the maze. They could only take about 30 minutes of being on their feet and they were exhausted. Ma too!

One nice usher by the name of McGill led Ma and me to a special room to rest. It had a big couch, a fireplace and a 50's television sets. We moved after a while to go the washroom and when Ma and I returned, other seniors had filled the special room we had left. We found seating in the hallway.

They were quiet and they reminded me of an old hymn, "I Am So Satisfied." As one senior said as she reflected on the gospel writers and singers, "Why shouldn't they honor our people? They have worked so hard!"

I felt so proud and so honored to be with them. I felt a strong connection to all that I am, for as Maya Angelou, "I'm the hope of the slave!" We stayed for only an hour. That's all that was required, for the elders were ready to go. When the bus came, we boarded. They were so at peace once seated. So was I. I will never forget how my mother lifted her eyes over the seat, looking for me since I was the last one to board the bus. They were the like the eyes of a child, searching for a familiar face. Blessed am I to have been in that number. And oh yeah, before I left the museum building, someone said, "Frederick Douglass is behind you." I thought, "Yeah right." But as I turned around, I saw a young man dressed as Frederick Douglass with a book in his hand. I said, "Hello, Mr. Douglass." He smiled.

As we all rode quietly back to the Hyde Park Neighborhood Club, the sun beamed down on all of us. Quiet joy! Hats off the Chicago Historical Society for honoring the historical figures of the gospel song and for giving our seniors an experience of a lifetime!

1/16/2000

MLK Day 2000 - #5

Today is MLK Jr., Day and many people were off from work. But I had to work and did not mind a bit. He said, "Be the best." As it would apply to me, he would say,"Be the best temp worker." And I did my best. I accomplished a lot.

When I first arrived at work, I felt that I had overdressed. I had on snow gear. Yet, around one o'clock, snow started to fall and it soon became a blizzard. It snowed for hours. As it turned out, I was in tune with Mother Nature's plan. I believe others were caught off guard

But with some trepidation about getting on my second bus, one stopped for the woman and me. We could barely squeeze on, but we made it. When I arrived at my building, one person was waiting to hold the door for me. How good it felt!

Then, when I arrived at my door, another neighbor had her door open and was cooking and offered a cheery hello. Interestingly, each person I encountered was of a different ethnicity. MLK, Jr's hard sacrifice was paying off,

Hats off to Dr. Martin Luther King, Jr.! It worked!!

1/17/2000

Tribute to: Dr. Martin Luther King, Jr.

You can't kill a dream,
You can only kill the dreamer.
And when you kill the dreamer
You give life to the dream
Because it brings attention to
What frightened you into
The suppression in the first place.
Certainly it makes generations
To come wonder and study
The power of the message.
That the dreamer brought
That no one can hush.

10/18/96
Memphis, TN

Lettie # 6

Before I forget, I must write about Lettie. Lettie is a 91- year old history lesson in the form of an African American woman. She is one of the seniors at the Hyde Park Neighborhood Club that I met that day I took the field trip with my mother and the group.

She said to me," If you go to sleep, I'm going to take your hair?" Her eyes lit up when she talked, but you could not really tell if she was looking at you or if she was blind. Obviously, she could see because she saw my hair.

Anyway, she said,"I am the oldest woman in this room." She did not look it. She had a tan color, with light or hazel eyes and thick white hair. It was parted down the middle and braided in two thick braids.

She was petite and still quite cute. She talked about her husband and said when she met him, he said he could not have kids. She chuckled, 'Chile, that man was full of babies! I had eight children!

When I looked at her, after we discovered that she was born in the county next to my mother's birthplace in Mississippi, so many comfortable feelings surged. Her ways and smooth way of talking reminded me of my Aunt Alma.

My Aunt Alma loved me and I loved her back. She lived in Mississippi and I used to visit her when I was in graduate school down there. I used to drive about 75 miles north of Jackson, to spend the weekends with her and my Uncle Robert.

Being around Lettie gave me an opportunity to revisit those sacred times and days. And I would guess that Lettie, just as Aunt Alma, was forced to move 'up North" with her kids once the husbands had passed on.

During the migration of African Americans to the north, some moves were wanted and some were forced due to conditions. It reminds me of Ernest Gaines' short story, "Just like a Tree." The matriarch had to leave the only home she knew and make do until that old setting sun came to meet her. However, she made other choices. But many women like Lettie, my mother and my Aunt Alma were widows who were at the mercy of their adult children who had to move and leave former lives behind.

Hats off to Lettie and all of the resilient seniors who chose to go with the flow and keep living.

1/17/2000

Lights! Action! #7

The other night while coming home from a temp assignment on North Michigan Avenue, I walked north, pass the Water Tower Place. People were busy trying to get home and the streets were blanketed with a fresh layer of snow.

As I looked around and noted the beautiful lights from the buildings and the quiet calm, I felt a sense of newness. Well, I thought, it is new- a new day, a new year in January and a new millennium.

As I walked along, trying to decide which route to take home, I ended up going in Borders Bookstore where I had heard and met the illustrious Alice Walker a few years earlier. Just being there felt good and it felt right. There was a subtle nudging that seemed to be saying, "Be patient. Your time will come. Just stay with it!"

I flowed through the bookstore, located a book that I wanted, purchased it and majestically went back outdoors into the crowd, caught my bus and headed home. I noticed the beautifully lit gazebo at Oak Street as the bus forged ahead. It made me feel like a child again- full of wonder, full of possibilities and inspired to stay the course!

Hats off to Chicago for the beautiful lighting that brings hope!

1/20/2000

Memory Lane- Wadsworth Elementary #8

Yesterday, I took a surprise walk down memory lane. I was riding with my sister and we ended up going through Woodlawn. When we came upon my old school, Wadsworth Elementary, I was truly caught off guard.

It is where I attended elementary school for one year in 1963. Our family had just arrived to Chicago and coming in from Memphis. I attended 8th grade there and many memories resurged throughout the day. That academic year altered my life forever.

I remember that day, when we were in front of the school passing out some type of boycott flyers or watching some students pass them out. I am not quite sure. But, I do recall that one of our classmates, Wilma walked up to us and told us that President Kennedy had been shot. It was a topsy-turvy day.

Later that day, I recall that the sky turned very dark and black and this was long before sundown. The whole night was filled with shock and mourning. I remember WVON continually played the song, "Open Our Eyes." Everyone was crying and I listened to that song over and over.

Those days at Wadsworth were really different days for me. This school was nothing like the warmth and friendships we had in the south. I felt no real camaraderie here. I remember when we were walking home one day, I witnessed a dehumanizing fight. A classmate, whom I liked and respected, was forced to fight a bully. They fought in the middle of the street. Her bra was snatched off during the fiasco and I was horrified for her. There were a lot of boys around and this was such a tender age for a growing teen

But on the lighter note, I met my friend Carolyn, who is still my friend today. I learned Chicago history from my teacher, Mrs. Moody. We,

Carolyn and I, had Mr. Boros, as our homeroom teacher. We both had a crush on him. She still has not forgiven me for fainting one day as I was being sketched by the class. I was standing on top of a desk as directed and I believe that the lights from the ceiling were too close and too hot. I blacked out. Mr. Boros caught me and to this day, Carolyn swears I staged it. Friends. Oh well.

But the stories could go on and on about this time in my life. At the time though, seriously, 63rd Street was filled with stores and had the noisy El train overhead. We used to start shopping at Stony Island and move all the way to Cottage Grove.

The highlights that I remember are Star Department Store, where Carolyn had her coerced fight. I stood guard to make sure no one else jumped in. I learned how things went quickly. I remembered Towne Shoes where one of my sisters worked; Jupiter; the two or three theatres such as the Les. I remember the bank, at the corner of 63rd and Woodlawn. I believe it was called Southeast Bank. I remember the bank because Wadsworth opened my first savings account for me after I gave the Farewell Speech at our 8th grade graduation.

As I look back, I was blessed. No one started a fight with me or really picked on me. I managed to stay under the radar. To set the musical backdrop, we had and still have Herb Kent, the Kool Gent. He is a Chicago deejay who played and plays all of the latest music. He and his colorful humor had us saying we were "Boss Fezneckies" which means you are a good-looking young lady.

It's funny how one structure that is still standing and healthily, can bring back so many wonderful and clear voices from the past. I still believe that attending Wadsworth gave me some insights into the urban life that my sisters don't have because they were older and did not attend that school. Wadsworth was my entrée into the real concrete jungle.

1/22/2000

Memory Lane- U of C's SWAP   # 9

When I was in my early teens and in 8th grade at Wadsworth Elementary, the University of Chicago came over and invited the girls to take a ballet class. I'll never forget those cold but dear mornings at Ida Noyes Hall on Saturdays. Our young teacher, probably a student, taught us the basics of modern dance. It was our first experience on the other side of Midway Plaisance, where we played either softball or ice skated during the winter. I remembered, mostly the warmth of the "hot houses" for I am no lover of winter sports.

Our relationship with the University of Chicago continued even after I started Hyde Park High School. There was an organization called SWAP that held dances for us teens. It gave me and my sisters a chance to walk the neighborhood of Hyde Park on a regular basis. We lived in Woodlawn. I recall noting the houses, condos, and apartments as we ventured to different functions.

When I think of SWAP, I have warm feelings of being on a campus atmosphere and having caring chaperones. One song that plays vividly in my mind is the Righteous Brothers' "You've Lost that Loving Feeling."

All of these early adventures were a sign of things to come. I did not know that I would spend many years in my later life, teaching on a variety of college campuses. I hope that these types of programs are still going on because you never know which persons are going to be greatly and positively influenced by those exposures.

Thanks to the University of Chicago for giving us SWAP. It gave us a safe haven and something positive to look forward to when less than positive things were sometimes happening on the other side the Midway Plaisance.

1/24/2000

Evanston #10

Upon revisiting Evanston last Friday, so many memories resurfaced. As my sister and I entered from Western Avenue, it reminded me of my old route home. I lived in Evanston and taught at Lane Tech for a couple of years in the mid 70's.

Evanston offered me a place to regroup and find new levels of inner peace after leaving the South Side of Chicago. I found a nice building on Oak Street and first, I rented the garden apartment. I later moved upstairs to the third floor and had a two- bedroom apartment. I remember the fireplace and truly remember my beloved pink rug that I had purchased.

After a few scary experiences on the South Side, I was again free in Evanston to find wholeness. I could ride my bike, go walking or even have the top down on my convertible Fiat Spider without fear of having unwanted company at the stop light.

I had gone there with hopes of enrolling into Northwestern University's School of Journalism, but that did not happen. However, so many other pleasant things did happen in my life in Evanston. I volunteered for the Evanston Review newspaper. I typed obits and dates & deadlines. It was a tedious task that I am sure no one else really wanted to do. I was allowed to do my first story for the paper. It was on child abuse because Evanston was chosen as one of 30 cities to be a pilot to start the discussion and exposure of child abuse. It is now a common topic but then it was an unspoken truth.

At the time, it was still a hush-hush situation. I conducted about six interviews with doctors and other professionals and did a lot of research at hospital libraries. I got my first by-line though the new incoming editor changed it quite a bit.

Anyway, along with that, teaching at Lane and working for the YMCA in the summer, I still found the time to be a cashier at Dominick's on the weekends. What was my goal? It was to pay off all of my debts because I could feel in my soul that I was to make my first exodus from Illinois and explore the great yonder.

And I did. I left there in May 1977, but before I left, I was able to take a Feature Story Writing class through the Continuing Education Department at Northwestern. I ended up with my second by- line and this one was on the beautiful Baha'i Temple. Again, I did a lot of research, read many books and visited the magnificent structure on several occasions.

As I prepared, a path did reveal itself and I returned to the sunny South for graduate school. I can truly say that Evanston offered me much. I left with two by-lines, a much greater inner peace and I was debt free. It had been a very rich experience and I will always have very warm feelings when I think of my time spent in Evanston – a true college town.

1/25/2000

63rd Street in '63 # 11

Before we left Memphis, Tennessee in May of 1963, my sisters cried and cried. I especially remember my older sister who had just graduated from Carver High in Memphis. I believe she had the hardest time because her friendships were more established. I remember her and her boyfriend, Willie Roy walking and walking up and down the streets, holding hands before we were commissioned to get into the car and leave for Chicago.

Anyway, the whole neighborhood seemed to be in tears as we loaded up in the car we called the "Bronze Bumble." Daddy had gotten it from Chicago and came back to Memphis to get us. He had gone there a month earlier and he found a job, got an apartment and bought a car. He returned to take us to our new home.

We left 1860 Benford Street and set out on our long sojourn. I remember him trying to assure us that we would love Chicago, but of course, we would have none of that! The only part of the long drive I remember was us losing the signal to the wonderful and soulful sounds of WDIA and WLOK from Memphis as we traveled further north. Also, we lost our luggage that was tied on top of the car. Daddy was driving along and some farmers kept signaling to us. When Daddy heeded the signals, we had to go back for it and fortunately it was along the side of the highway. Also, in those segregated days, if we had to go the bathroom, we would stop along the side of the road. We hated it, but my mother would orchestrate and talk us through the whole process.

When we finally arrived in Chicago, it was Memorial Day in 1963. I remember because that holiday is not truly celebrated in the South. When we drove towards our new apartment, we headed north on Stony Island. I recall seeing people sleeping on the park bench around 63rd street at

Jackson Park. As I watched through the car window in disbelief, I did not see how this could turn out well.

We made it to 6140 S. Kenwood. The apartment was upstairs and it was a nice four room place. To me, Daddy had done an excellent job of laying things out for us. Those were my feelings then and I still feel that way today.

As we settled in, we made many friends among the neighborhood children. There were the Lawsons, the Lewises and the Threadgills to name a few. Some of those friendships have remained some 40 plus years later.

And of course, we had to do laundry, buy groceries and handle daily business; so we were introduced to the almighty 63rd Street. It was topped by the noisy Jackson Park El train. It was absolutely amazing to me when I thought of those people who actually had apartments right on the same level as those tracks.

But the awesome part was what was going on under the el train. There was constant movement among the people. There were grocery stores, large and small shops, theatres, department stores, banks, shoe stores, laundry mats. You name it. All the way to King Drive, then called South Park, there was a plethora of businesses.

I witnessed so many levels and degrees of life. But I think that the biggest disturbance to me were all of the confused people. I wondered what could happen to a person to make them lose total sight of who they were. I had to observe so many men dressed like women in their clothes with feathers and the whole nine yards. And then there were the reasonable number of women dressed as men. What we called them then would be considered to be 'politically incorrect' today. This truly baffled me as a 12-year old!

There was never a dull moment on 63rd Street. There were grown people fighting under the viaduct; a man switching like a woman, a woman with a process and dressed in a man's suit. There were long lines waiting for the liquor store to open once and when inquiring about why, I found out it was Election Day and it had been closed for the earlier hours. Whew.

I never recall feeling any fear for my safety. There was just always some live action as people carried on about what they perceived as their normal lives.

1/25/2000

Wheaton College #12

In the summer of 1993, I spent the summer at Wheaton College. I had just finished a stint as a lecturer with Chicago State University. I was then offered a position as an English Teacher through the University's Upward Bound Program.

Upward Bound is a program designed to introduce at -risk or culturally deprived students to life on a college campus, with the hopes that they would one day choose to attend one. I had worked with an Upward Bound program in the summer of 1980 at Ohio Wesleyan University and strongly believed in its mission to assist inner city youth in gaining exposure and in seeking new horizons.

So, I packed up my car, left my apartment in Chicago Heights and headed to Wheaton, Illinois. I had never lived on a college campus other than the time I did the Upward Bound Program in Delaware, Ohio with Ohio Wesleyan. There, in Ohio, three of us shared a gigantic frat house and had several rooms apiece. In Wheaton, I had a suite in a dormitory which consisted of two adjoining rooms and a private bathroom.

I made one room into a study and the other one was my bedroom. The girls we were supervising were down the hall and surprisingly I do not remember any major incidents with them in the dormitory that summer. I taught about four or five classes a day, taught modern dance in a dance room full of mirrors and I assisted in afterschool homework.

Mostly, I remember the absolutely great food in the cafeteria. I recall the long walks around the campus with a friend and staffer named Jim. We talked as we solved all of the world's problems.

I felt a great sense of peace there. I remember the greenery, the trees and the quaintness of this university town. I felt safe and sometimes, I was so involved with students' learning and affairs that I forgot what was going on in the world. We did not have access to television in our rooms, as this was done by design. One day, I looked up and noticed a television out in the meeting area and saw the pictures of all the serious flooding that was taking place in downstate Illinois.

Other than that, our total involvement was focused on the students and the academic program at hand. Once, after an emotional eruption with a student, in the classroom, I walked over to one of the campus churches for a reprieve. I needed to calm down and it just so happened that I sat next to the minister's wife.

She asked me what I needed and I explained to her that I was an English teacher that was working with inner city youth for the summer on that campus. I told her that I had just been verbally assaulted. She took my hand, asked me my name and said that she would give it to her husband, the minister. He was reading a letter from the book of Isaiah when the prophet had learned of a plot to destroy his life. It talked about how he chose to lay the letter before God. He was going to allow God to work it out. I left the church feeling that a burden had been lifted and was able to return to work and proceed with ease.

What I also remember most of that summer in Wheaton is the greenery and the sacredness of the setting. The walks, the jogging court and shopping in the downtown area added to my rich memories. A co-worker, Mina, bought me some black ballet shoes as a gift for driving her around. I bought myself some pink stretch pants that originally costs $70. I bought them on sale for about $30, and counted myself lucky.

Once, I drove Mina and myself to Glen Ellyn to the show. We wanted to get away from the campus, which we were allowed to do on weekends. The students often went home and sometimes, I went back to my apartment in Chicago Heights as well. That was a nice little drive.

Overall, Wheaton was an extremely rich experience. Teaching the students further reading and writing skills, visiting the campus library and getting videos on famous African Americans' lives all combined to help them and to also further enrich me. The theme around the entire summer was the Underground Railroad and we discovered that Wheaton had once served as one of its stations. At the end of the summer, I felt that I had fulfilled Maya Angelou's line from *And Still I Rise* and had become the "hope of the slave."

2/21/2000

Angles # 13

Today, I am sitting here in my rocking chair angled at a position that I have not used in my apartment on North LaSalle. I am seeing things outside my window that I had not noticed before now.

It is sunny and I can see a huge white crane that stands taller than the buildings. Even though it is President's Day, the men are at work. Of course, I don't know what they are working on because I do not know all about construction. But I did see a huge yellow wrecking ball, so perhaps they are about to demolish something. It could be over by Cabrini, but I cannot tell for sure. I decided to pull out my binoculars and saw that it was not a wrecking ball, but a huge pulley to transfer equipment.

Anyway, this scene is significant to me because I just fought to keep my apartment and I just discovered its beauty from a new "point of view." Sometimes, we have to take what we have and reconfigure it; turn it over; shake it up and see the blessings from another angle! It's all in how you look at it, in this life.

2/21/2000

Cathedral – Used #14

When I was teaching at Prairie State College a few years back, I taught a short story entitled, "Cathedral' by Carver. I believe that was author's last name. Anyway, when I looked out of my window, if I adjust the position of my rocker, I can see a beautiful cathedral.

It is brown brick with a white dome and it seems as though it has green on the steeple. But of course, most significantly, it has a cross on top. It means so very much to me. It reminds me that God is still on the throne when my faith in man is wavering. It reminds me to look up and out and not down.

At night, when I look out at the Cathedral, the lights are always on in the "upper room." So inspiring! It reminds me of one of Mahalia Jackson's song, *In the Upper Room*. Also, the other tall item I see is a white columnar saying, "Used." Put the two together and I would say the equation is: "*The cathedral* is *used by many*-even by those who do not enter the structure. Just seeing the steeple or the lit upper room offers solace and comfort to many weary travelers and seekers.

2/21/2000

Brother Isley #15

The other night, my sister and I attended an Isley Brothers Concert, though there was actually only one Isley Brother performing there. It was at the Chicago Theatre, where I had gone many times in my teens and young adult years to see movies.

Now, it has been transformed into a theatre for live performances. As we entered, so many memories of its layout came back to me. Once our tickets were taken, we passed through the throngs of people standing around "stylin' and profilin', seeing who's who and who they knew.

As we proceeded to our seats and walked down the decline, I remembered years before, while on a date, I didn't know that the walkway sloped down and I fell flat on my face. People seated around started laughing. Needless to say, this was a most embarrassing moment.

I quickly shared that memory with my sister the other night as I cautiously went to my seat. First on stage, there was a young group called "Mint Condition." Of course, I did not know their songs and truly was reminded that I am now middle-aged. The people of their age group clapped and sang every line with them. One young woman with a lot of hair had gone completely wild, bobbing up and down on their second tune.

My sister said, "Grace Poole." I said, "It's too early in the concert for her to be this happy. Perhaps she came in happy or had some help."

"Yeah, she is in another place," my sister responded. The group, Mint Condition, was good.

We were later invited backstage to meet them. The route we took to go backstage was a long, treacherous cave-like thoroughfare. We were led by some of the employees there and for a moment, we thought this was some type of joke.

We finally came to a 'clearing" and ended up in a reception room with mirrors, pictures of the group, chairs and light food. The group finally came into the room. We stood, shook their hands and some of us even took pictures with them. As we were cordially engaged in conversation with the group, I heard the Isley Brothers' song called "Between the Sheets." I did not want to seem rude, but I wanted to "go."

These were the songs that reminded me of my younger years and who we had actually come to see. This was the main attraction. I voiced that and eventually we were led back through the tunnel that had pipes hanging low and you had to bend down to avoid.

We were glad when we opened the door from that spooky adventure and saw that we were back in the lower part of the theatre with 'familiar surroundings.' As we re-entered the theatre, there stood the youngest, I believe, brother of the Isley Brothers. He had on a pink suit and had a ponytail. He had a cane and wore what looked liked black and white spats for shoes. It was Ronnie Isley, all alone.

Interestingly, he took us through 40 years of songs from *Twist and Shout* from 1959; *it's Your Thang* from 1969; and on and on. The ones that have played in my head since that night are *Summer Breeze; Nothing but Smooth Sailing* and his extremely special rendition of *All I do is Cry*. With this one, he actually got on his knees and truly played the part of a love sick man.

He reminded us that he wore pink for Valentine's Day which was the following Monday. I noticed that he kept his eyes closed as he sang and I mentioned it to my sister. She said, "Maybe if he opens his eyes he might stop singing." Interesting observation!

But at the end of the concert, he did let us (or shall I say me) see his beautiful eyes. The concert was a grand experience and I shall always remember it. I felt so honored and blessed to see this Isley Brother sing.

As we filed out, the throngs of people were growing thick again. People were speaking of a coat check line and I could see this could turn into a real herd. I looked up and saw an usher who assured us that we could use the side exit to avoid the crowd on State Street. We did and exited out on Lake Street.

Thank God! We got out with no hassle and I thought,"It all comes back, just like riding a bicycle." Those are deeply etched memories of the Chicago Theatre from both the past and the present. All good!

2/21/2000

Buckingham Fountain   #16

As I sit here staring at the Buckingham Fountain, I was reminded of walking in the Garden of Tuileries in Paris, France.   There was also a fountain towards the end of the walk and it reminded me of that spring trip. The days were similar in mildness of weather which offered so many pleasantries.

When I saw a traveler taking pictures, it reminded me of the Frenchman who took my picture. He asked," Are you an American?" After I said yes, he rubbed down my hair and took my picture there by the fountain on a cloudy March day in 1996.

Looking at the Buckingham also reminded me of freedom. I felt and feel free. When I look to the east, I see Lake Michigan. It is a display of God in all of His glory. And when I look to the west, I see skyscrapers. Man and all of his competitive sport,

The fountain is not on, but it's great to be out in the wide, blue yonder. Oh, to breathe God's air is so divine! Looking at the dry structure of the Fountain, you try to imagine how anyone could build such a magnificent structure. It was a gift to Chicago from Kate Buckingham in memory of her brother Clarence. What a mighty gesture of love! It just reminded me that my concerns are miniscule and bigger and grander things are being accomplished every day in so many ways.

2/22/2000

A Sitting Lincoln # 17

In all of the years I have spent in Chicago, I had never noticed this statue of President Lincoln sitting. It is situated to the south of the Art Institute between Michigan and Columbus and south of the Jackson Street overpass. It is not visible from either of those streets, so if you are not walking you would not come upon the statue of Lincoln sitting down.

The statue seems to be bronzed and his head is tilted downward as if he is in a prayerful or meditative position. It made me think of the heavy burden and pain he carried as he witnessed the country being torn apart during the Civil War. His grief and responsibility were immense.

Spiritually so, today's message from *Today in the Word* , spoke of his life and how he faced so much ridicule. I am sure that he had to have experienced a lot of pain in his lifetime. Not only did he witness the death of thousands of young soldiers, he also had to endure the loss of his own son during his presidency.

The other time I visited a Lincoln statue that was "standing," I was in Springfield, Illinois. I felt we had a mystical conversation as I stood before his tall statue. I finally sat there next to him, at his feet and sat in the silence.

So here I am, the day after President's Day during his birth month, looking at a statue of a man who left his mark on this country. Those here, those who have gone on and certainly those to come all have or will benefit from his great life. Thanks, Abraham Lincoln, for having been born! Also, Happy Birthday to George Washington on this date- his true birthday!

2/22/2000

And Mad About It! # 18

Here I am looking at the 'displaced lion.' As I was walking pass the Art Institute, I saw one of the lions that has been in place since 1874, had been moved! It had made the news. He had been moved for a renovation project.

He's now sitting to the north of the entrance of the Art Institute in a cage in a little garden. I started to stop and write about it, but to me he looked a little, ticked off. However, they were kind enough to explain his temporary move on the news and on a plaque attached to the cage in which he stood.

If he's been guarding the Art Institute since 1874, and Chicago itself, surely yon cannot explain renovation to him. He's probably thinking, well why did my partner get to stay in his permanent location?

As in life, he doesn't know that his partner's turn to be moved, shuffled around and caged is definitely coming. And when they are both back in their old places, they will have a deeper understanding and appreciation for the sure things.

Besides, just in the five minutes I have been here, several people have come to stare at him, take his picture and just gawk. Though he is mad about it, he is getting more attention now, than he did before the move. Isn't that life?

2/22/2000

Open Learning #19

As I walked north of Michigan Avenue and approached the Art Institute, I saw a group of students sitting on a bench. One was standing with papers in hand, probably making a presentation to the others.

It brought a warm feeling because education seems to do that to me. But the participants seemed so willingly attentive. That was the beauty of it. They were open and willing to receive.

It reminded me again of my trip to Paris in 1996 when I found myself of the Sorbonne. I observed the students as they, too, studied in an outdoor scene in a park across the street from the entrance to the university. Again, it was around the same time of year when hints of spring were in the air and being in the outdoors was a grand blessing.

And, as I reached the other side of the Art Institute where the caged lion sits, there too was a group of students studying and presenting to one another. Oh, the joy of learning, if you make it so! If only all students could be open and receptive, there would be a lot of happy learners!

2/22/2000

Chicago Mounties #20

Today, I was standing at the corner of Clark and Elm waiting on the bus. The weather was beautiful and I looked up and saw two mounted policemen approaching on two beautiful horses!

As they came closer, I felt honored to be so close to these wonderful creatures. The policemen sat tall and proud in the saddle. They seemed very glad to be on the horses rather than in the mundane car, on bike or even deeper, on foot.

The saddles had Chicago Police Department flapped down on the sides. It was a glorious sight to behold. As they moved pass, almost close enough to touch, a car with Michigan tags pulled up and asked one of the policemen, "Which way is the lake?"

One officer proceeded to give the driver directions and in another instant, the mounted policemen were gone. It all happened so quickly, but it gave me such a warm feeling to be that close to those beautiful horses. And to see some happy Chicago policemen was also a very good thing to see on a sunny day in the city.

3/4/2000

The Fisherman at Oak Street Beach #21

Today, I walked to the lakefront to clear my mind after dealing with some pretty heady stuff. It was about 65 degrees in March and an absolutely beautiful day for the Windy City. I felt my father's presence as a form of comfort and wondered what advice he would have given me in this matter concerning the family, had he still been alive.

Anyway, as I walked along Oak Street Beach, there was a picturesque view of the lake. People were jogging, riding bikes, walking dogs and just enjoying the wonderful weather. Finally, after keeping pace with others, I decided to sit down on the bricks. At one end, a middle-aged couple, was sitting and talking to each other. They took turns resting their heads on one another's shoulders and seemed very intimate. I loved it!

There were also tourists that had other passersby take their pictures. Then there was another peaceful couple to the other side of me as well. But what I most noticed, which is why I was drawn to that location, was a man fishing! In Lake Michigan!! He had a chair, pails and the whole nine yards!

His presence reminded me of my father who loved to fish. It also reminded me of a picture I took of Daddy fishing in a small pond outside my apartment in Georgia. I leaned over my balcony and took a picture of him fishing with all his gear in place. It was where he found solace.

So, now I made the connection. Seeing this fisherman at the Oak Street Beach made me break my stride and take a seat. I watched him as he reeled in something and it was the most comforting twenty minutes. It could have been Daddy's way of saying, "Breathe and relax."

Finally, I got up and asked the couple to my right "Is it legal to fish in Lake Michigan?"

The man responded, "Yes, but I don't know about here; but, I think it is great!"

My response, "Oh, I love it! I just hadn't seen anyone else do it!"

So, as I walked back to my apartment, I felt that I had been revisited my father. Earlier that morning, a letter he had written some years earlier had fallen out of my Bible and I had re-read it. I knew that he had heard my woeful cries. Seeing the fisherman at Oak Street Beach let me know that his spirit was touching mine.

3/4/2000

Happy Birthday, Chicago *#22*

On Sunday morning, my mother, sister and I were in the car heading west on Chicago Avenue. As we approached Michigan, I looked over to the Water Tower and saw big black plastic ribbons hanging from the structure. There hung a big sign saying, "Happy Birthday, Chicago." It had the birth year of 1837.

It was a comforting sight, seeing the celebration sign hanging on one of the few sites left from the Great Chicago Fire. It is always good to see the City of Chicago in all of its glory when you have to skirt around the darker issues of big cities. Again, this day was sunny. It was the Sabbath and mostly, my mother enjoyed the view as well.

It was quite uplifting to the spirit when you have been caged up for the winter. It was surely a positive and happy sign displayed on that day on the Magnificent Mile.

3/6/2000

Lunch at the Wrigley Building #23

Yesterday, I worked in the Wrigley Building for a temp agency. Of course, it is one of the most beautiful buildings in the Chicago Loop. It is where I currently bank and where my aunt used to bank.

Anyway, the weather was in the 70's which was a true sign of spring, after a dismal winter. I went out for lunch and sat on the concrete wall before the entry to the river walk. People were everywhere, eating outside, frolicking, talking, reading and basically just enjoying the sun. Some were peering over the ledge at the Chicago River.

A lot of them were probably employees from the Sun Times, the Wrigley Building itself and only heaven knows from where else. I found a small space on the wall and took out my sandwich and enjoyed every bite with every breath of fresh air. It was good to see people so peaceful and relaxed during their mid-day break.

I felt happy to be in the midst of peace. I breathed and smiled, so I enjoyed my lunch outside of the specially-shaped, ivory white Wrigley Building of Chicago.

3/7/2000

Hyde Park High School   #24

The other day, we drove pass Hyde Park High School, my alma mater. As I looked over in the school's direction, all of the voices from the mid-60's came flowing back to me. First, when I looked over at the sunken area of Jackson Park, across the street from the school, its many uses replayed in my mind.

On several very early mornings, we used to practice for marching band with the band director, Mr. Shannon. He would holler out maneuvers and holler if the sounds were not coming out right. He was a 'hollerer," but we loved him just the same.

The most memorable highlight was a parade in which we marched and played going down 63rd Street. I played flute and my partner, Leila marched along side me. We were second flutes, not first; but we had fun. We probably just blew a lot of wrong notes because we were very aware of the eyes of the onlookers as we tried to keep the marching steps and the reading of the music synchronized.

Our band uniforms never did fit and we never could afford new ones, but we enjoyed every moment. Some of the band uniform skirts had been hemmed over and over. Once, Leila and I caught the el train all the way to Austin High School. We had to catch several trains and it seemed to take an eternity to get there. We were traveling there to play in a band competition and we played a duet. I am sure the judges thought we were just mediocre, but we didn't get too embarrassed. We were having a new adventure and we had the courage to do it,

Shifting scenes, Jackson Park also served as a place for rare outside classes, a mating ground, and a place to cut classes when defying the teachers during the rebellious sixties or for the various sports teams' practices. The park was extension of the school and was always filled with some activity that was school-related.

The inside of the school was another experience. Things within the school were quite orderly and well-run. Our assistant principal, Ms, S kept law and order. She was very small in stature but ruled with an iron fist. If the word got out, and it traveled fast, that she was in the hallway, many of us just went another way. Some of us did not want to take a chance on a confrontation. We feared and greatly respected her. She was the sheriff of the day!

I flowed through four years at Hyde Park High with no major interruptions. I had all honors classes in a tracking system that had basic, essential, regular, honors, high honors and advanced placement. There were very few in the advanced placement track and most of them started their academic day very early in the morning and left early. Basically, we moved in small circles and traveled with the students who were on the same track.

I had a special interest in my English classes, my English teachers and their teaching styles. I was nurtured by Ms. J, as a freshman and remember studying *Romeo and Juliet* and compiling an Egyptian mythology scrapbook. Ms. H challenged my writing abilities in my sophomore year but the junior year was lost in disappointment because our teacher was already burned out. But, my senior year made up for it with Ms. Mc. She was a delight and I recall reading *Miss Julie* and *Hamlet*. Her ability to bring out the hidden symbols in literature helped me later decide to become an English major and English teacher myself.

Hyde Park was a school filled with little cliques. One needed friends to survive the otherwise isolation. And, I had my close friends, Pen and Bren and we were called the 'threesome." In '67, our cheerleaders were the state champions and they made us extremely proud during the grim days of the Vietnam War. They were also very close friends and sang the song S-U-C-C-E-S-S- that's the way we spell success. Those words kept us going and helped us persevere during those years when our upper classmen and recent graduates were being drafted and our class size diminishing.

The stories could go on endlessly, but I feel that I learned a lot first academically for we prided ourselves on being ranked as 17th in the nation at that time. I learned culture and class for the school was a mixed bag of the children of the University of Chicago employees and the children from the mean streets of Woodlawn. From this, I learned how to survive and how to observe more and stay out of harm's way. Some students were making poor choices such as experimenting with drugs such as LSD and others were making great choices that landed them great careers. It was truly a memorable four years at Hyde Park High and I will always cherish my time spent there!

3/9/2000

The Frenchman   #25

During my stint on a former temp job, I met a Frenchman who shall remain nameless. He was from Paris and I was intrigued because I had been there fairly recently. I have always been interested in the French language and culture after taking years of French from four different teachers.

To digress, Ms. N from high school concentrated on the conjugation of verbs and listening to recorded dialogues. In college, the instructor talked about the country and its geography and the culture mostly. Many years later, I had a professor from Senegal that used interesting techniques in teaching the language.   She was very enthusiastic and drew us in. We held on to her every word and tried hard to please her. And last, I had a Madame W who taught "Conversational French." This, I believe, better prepared me to think about traveling to France. I needed to know how to communicate initially, not conjugate verbs or know the French map.

So, I go back to the Frenchman on the job. His cubicle was across from mine we *had* to communicate to a degree. He seemed withdrawn and isolated and somewhat angry. I, too, was quite angry at the time because I felt that life had dealt me a series of unwarranted blows. But, then there were always wonderful co-workers that brought laughter and made me forget my own inner woes.

There was one such woman named Paula who could make anyone laugh. Paula, the Frenchman and I ended up communicating daily. Together, we helped each other break down some of the barriers and blocks. The fact that I had traveled to Paris helped him open up to me a bit and Paula's hilarious antics helped him relax. I imagine he felt isolated because the other guys in the office did not seem to be reaching out to him either.

When the atmosphere was more relaxed and he felt that he could trust us, I was surprised to hear him say that I used to "go off on him every Monday." He had it timed! I felt that he needed a little new adaptation to the American woman because before he was quite arrogant and would say just whatever- without thinking.

But over the period of a year and a half, we grew. He became much more positively interactive with his colleagues and was less withdrawn. I also learned from him when he would remind me to "just go with the flow." He, too, had softened.

He had a proud, upright walk. As a song said, "He walked like an Egyptian." And I believe that he was a bit of a rebel. If he felt that things were wrong, he did not hesitate to speak his mind on the issue, even regarding his beloved France. I remember that he was watching the World Cup Soccer Tournament, and when France won, he was ecstatic. I had never seen him show that type of emotion.

I learned a lot about France from listening to him. He explained how their school system worked and I compared it to ours. We exchanged. When he could see that I was having a rough day, he gently nudged me into a lighter mood and the day got better. For example, this was during the time that JFK, Jr's plane disappeared. He knew how upset I had been and the next day at work, he broke it to me gently and told me that they had found the three bodies and the aircraft. The way we he did it made it easier to accept.

He had the roar of a lion but the heart of a lamb. I used to love hearing him having conversations on the phone in French. Just hearing the musical sound of the language was like listening to a song. Of course, I did not know what he was saying. I recall him saying *Merry Christmas* and *Happy Birthday* in French to me.

When they moved my cubicle, as a typical Frenchman, he protested very loudly. But we had strengthened each other, after straightening each other out and I will always cherish my time spent with the Frenchman. I believe that we truly helped each other cope with the world and the ways of the world.

3/10/2000

The Wendella Boat Ride   #26

At the end of the summer of 1998, I took my first Wendella Boat Ride. I had not planned on it, but the thought of returning to my restrictive living conditions at the time overwhelmed me. I was standing by the Wrigley Building waiting for the bus and I looked down and saw people sitting on the boat. Some were still boarding, so I rushed down the winding stairs, quickly paid at the booth and was the last person to board before the boat left the dock.

We started out by heading west on the Chicago River. The day was mild and sunny. To the left of me, I saw some type of fishing event going on. I recalled how me and a couple of my former co-workers years earlier used to leave work in the Loop and go and sit down by the river during that summer stint.

The boat then passed the beautiful green building at 333 West Wacker where I was working at the time. We turned with the river's bend and passed the Standard Oil Building. The woman, tour guide, explained different historic sites in a rather rapid speed. I filtered in what I could and tried to clear some of the debris from my own mind.

Basically, I noticed the skill of the skipper. He was strong and able, and it was interesting to see him operate so efficiently in an occupation I had never witnessed before that boat ride. As others boats passed, we all waved to one another as we took in the awesome views of the Chicago skyscrapers from new points of view.

The boat then turned around and we headed back towards the bend close to Merchandise Mart and headed back east. I thought the ride was nearly over, but then we bypassed the Wrigley Building where we had embarked. Little did I know that the best was yet to come. We headed towards the grand and blue Lake Michigan.

We halted. The skipper secured the boat. There was a gate that acted as a stop light. We had to wait on our turn for entry. Then the most incredible thing happened. The boat started rising up in the water. Everybody stood up to see what was happening. It was like nothing that I had ever experienced.

We were there by a lighthouse. On top, there was a seagull perched as if to say, "Don't worry. I got you." This was a good omen and spiritual sight because I love lighthouses and respect the birds.

When the gates opened, we were on the higher level to flow out into the majestic Lake Michigan. I had never been out on the lake though it has always played a role in my life in some way. We went out into the lake for quite a distance. We first headed north on the lake. As the city diminished, it seemed that I was able to put the whole city into perspective. It was like minimizing a screen on a computer. I could compare man's structures to God's splendor!

For a moment, I could stand back, away from my own inner dilemmas and put things into their proper order. I could see what was monumental and what was truly small. I regained my composure and felt that I knew what I needed to do when I returned back to land.

The boat turned around and we headed south on the lake. We came close to the rear of the Shedd Aquarium where I could plainly see the Oceanarium, which I have not visited. Then, we headed back towards the Chicago River. When we approached the gates, the boat descended to meet the water levels of the river. Now, we understood what was happening as the boat started lowering.

The Wendella Boat ride was a real adventure. I was so taken with the vastness of it all that I was basically unaware of my fellow passengers. We ended back up a little further south of the Wrigley Building and unloaded, climbed the steps and ended back into the real work.

My head had cleared some. I was better able to go back to those restrictive living conditions, take charge and make changes. I moved shortly afterwards. Just as the gates let us onto the larger Lake Michigan, the boat ride helped me to open my mind and know that there was truly more freedom and better ways of living. I give thanks for hopping on the Wendella Boat ride that day and will always remember what it did to open my mind and the doors to greater opportunity. What a treat!

3/18/2000

Gold Coat Suites #27

I moved into Gold Coast Suites because I needed, as Virginia Woolf said, "A room of my own." I had been living with others for over two years, so that little suite looked like heaven to me. I was told a flight attendant had just stayed there and of the choices, this one had a warm feeling. It had furnishings and mostly, it was a room with a view.

When I looked out, I could see west on Division Street. I was on the top floor so to me, it was my own little penthouse. I moved in right before the holidays so I could always hear laughter from the people enjoying the pubs and enjoying life. I never felt alone.

In the mornings, I could see the people stirring and moving around and I knew that life was truly going on. This was so important to me at that time. It was a reminder that "life truly goes on," and so do we, if we choose.

Outside my window, I could see people scurrying to the Starbucks, Walgreens and even guys selling *Streetwise* on the corners. I could truly count my blessings in this less than perfect world. And of course, I could see the church. To myself, I said, "l'eglise" which is French for church. I knew that was a good sign and vowed to attend. I did. I walked and attended regularly to find an anchor in my ever-changing life.

The sounds of the fire trucks, the non-stop traffic, the brisk walking pedestrians and the laughter coming from the bars and pubs reminded me that life had not slowed down. The loud music and the late celebrations of St. Patrick's Day let me know that it was still a beautiful world.

This strip had every convenience anyone could ever need to make it. There was Jewel's grocery store, Walgreen's, Osco, the Gap, a Boston Market and plenty of modes of transportation whether it was bus, cab or train- all right there. And the beach was in walking distance along with bookstores and restaurants galore.

And, most importantly, I had people looking out for me. The staff, mostly guys, the guard at the Gap all had an extra set of eyes knowing that I basically went to work, came in and wasn't seen too often until the next day. Now when I am in that area and I look up at #1204, my suite, I smile. I am thankful for that place of refuge where I stayed until I could, as the song says, get "Back on my feet again!" Thanks to the Gold Coast Suites who welcomed this weary traveler. As Wayne Dyer said, "We should bless our roofs and shelters."

3/18/2000

For Hazel (Ma)

I saw many stars in the sky when I woke up yesterday morning,
But then I witnessed a constellation with an intricate pattern.
Like Hazel.
She never left your life the same.
She was a messenger. A jewel; a pearl of wisdom.
Always taking you to a deeper level of thought.
Whether through a book, a quote, a parable or a story.
Such a great storyteller!
A great conversationalist.
Responding in kind with a joke, a nod, and a look.
You always walked away pondering. Thinking.
Firm, strong, feisty, upright and straight forth.
Not a *huggy, huggy, kissy, kissy*
But a realist.
A Rock.
Standing.
Shining. Waiting for you to get the lesson.
The blessing.
From a star teacher.

12/27/02
Chicago, IL

(Upon my mother's passing on December 24, 2002)

Shelter in Boston –2000

In June 2000, I arrived in Boston on an Amtrak train coming in from the Big Apple. I had spent about three months in NYC working as a temp for a dot.com company and living in a weekly in Lower Manhattan. I was there when the dot.com crash was manifesting, so with my last check, I bought a train ticket and headed for Boston, where I knew no one.

I was an aspiring writer, with my manuscript in tow and in search for a publisher or at least a literary agent. I had put my things in storage in Chicago and headed to an area where I believed I could make some connections and at least have a historical literary walk.

When I got off the train at South Station, the sun was shining though we had come through some cloudy, dismal weather on the way. I was so excited! For a moment, I just sat on one of wooden benches and just swung my feet as though I was a little girl again. My soul was singing, "I'm in Boston! I'm in Boston."

As a former high school English teacher, it had been a dream of mine to walk the grounds where the literary giants walked, wrote and talked. But joy soon gave way to despair as I remembered that I did not know anyone, did not know where I would sleep and had a very low cash flow.

I had decided the course of action on the train, so I tried to remain calm as a walked over to the phones, found the phonebooks and looked up the church of my aunt's affiliation, which now is mine also. As the kind woman answered the phone, I started to tell her my dilemma. My voice grew more panicky and shrill as the saga unraveled.

She gave quick, decisive directions and gave me the names and numbers of a shelter for women. I made the phone call, was given the green light and took a cab with my luggage to the first point of help.

I was given a meal with some very concerned servers, transferred to another shelter and thus spent my first night in Boston, still excited and still in a state of disbelief. That night I gave away tons and tons of clothes. I had already left coats and items with a person working in the hotel in New York, but I knew that if you wanted to travel far, you had to travel light.

The next morning, I left, as we all did. I walked and wandered a little and all along the way, people stopped and gave aid and eventually directed me to a better shelter. I came to Pine Street Inn for Women on that day and compared to where I had been, it looked like if not heaven, certainly a haven, until I could get my bearings.

I was quickly admitted, given a locker for my worldly possessions, the policies and procedures and thus began my five-month stay at this location. I was given the name of a temp agency where I could pick up my pay and not have the hassle of "your check is in the mail" syndrome. After daily walks, pounding the pavement, looking and searching, the agency put me to work. The agency sent me to a Talbot store, a temp agency as a receptionist and then to a law firm where I was able to work in the call center and build my revenue.

On my off days, I had a map of the city and I walked and walked and explored the many treasures both hidden and unhidden. It was a time when the tall ships were coming in and being a Midwesterner, any thing on the water brought about excitement.

The women at Pine Street Inn came in all shapes, sizes and ages and colors. Various circumstances had brought each of us to this crossroad in our lives. About five of us formed an unnamed network. We were the working women, who were in the Working Women's Program. We were somewhat privileged because we automatically had beds when we returned from work. We did not have to participate in the daily lottery for beds. Once the beds were gone you had to go to another shelter, certainly not as clean or well kept.

Some of the women had very grave issues and could not work. Some had had drug addictions or drinking problems. Some had had abusive spouses or mates and several had lost custody of their children, so any laughter was a blessing!

When we got in from work, the first thing we'd do is go to the garden, light up a cigarette and unload about the work day or whatever. It was the best place for free therapy in the world. There you were talking with women who knew nothing about you but what you told them. They could not check your story and rarely thought to judge you. We were too busy trying to put our own lives back together and move on to the next phase.

What saved me was reading books from the library and the public library. They called me the voracious reader. Also, there was laughter and the comical figures which might dot the landscape at any minute. Of course, there were those who had just about crossed over to the other side right in front of your face. And then, there was the music. What would we do without the music?

We all had headphones and a radio. That summer, I believe that the Backstreet Boys and Mark Anthony truly gave my heart a real lift and put the sun in fun. There was joy inside our pain and less fear of the next thing.

I did save over a thousand dollars to move into a YWCA in South Boston. In the fall, I moved into my own room after five months of shared space. I got nice cards and gifts and my entire group did move on into their own spaces. A year later, I went on to rent a condo in Back Bay for over two years.

I look back and say I didn't get the publisher or literary agent, but I received *so much more*. Kahil Gibran, who was one of the literary greats of Boston, wrote, "Keep me away from the wisdom which does not cry, the philosophy which does not laugh and the greatness which does not bow before children." He, too, spoke of the refuge he found in Boston and it is inscribed on a monument in Copley Square.

6/2006
Chicago, IL

Newberry Library Writing Workshop

Free write #1

The facilitator had us close our eyes and smell something that she put under our noses. We wrote about what emotions flourished from the scent. I wrote:

The smell reminds me of cinnamon. When I think of this smell, I am reminded my childhood. For some reason, it reminded me of Christmas and my mother's cooking. I probably thought of Christmas because that's when she cooked all of her specialties. Also, I thought of cinnamon toast. It is made by sprinkling cinnamon on a buttered piece of bread and toasting it lightly.

This smell brought pleasantries to mind. It is funny how smells and aromas can take you to certain places in time or even reawaken some past experience that we have tucked away in a sacred place. Colognes, fragrances and sweet smells can bring old cherished memories to life and make us recall how good times are only a thought away.

3/2009

Free write #2

After being given a piece of candy, I wrote:

Sucking on caramel candy, I am transported back to another chapter of my childhood. Again, I pull out another scene from those long gone days. When I was about eight years old, my three sisters and I used to walk to the Southgate Shopping Center in Memphis.

When we went to the mall, we always visited a drug store called Katz. It had a big cat face as a logo on the outside of the store. I distinctly remember going to the candy counter and in those days, the lady who worked there would measure out the amount of candy you wanted or in our case the amount we could afford. She would use a large silver cup to measure the amount and put it on a scale. You would then get your own individual bag. This was before the pre-packaged candy days.

Anyway, the caramel candy was always one of my choices. My sisters and I all had different tastes and made varying decisions at the candy counter. Yet, we would later share at least one piece of our candy with one other. Those were good memories. The lengthy walk and the purchasing power all added to the delight of the taste of the candy.

3/2009

Free write #3

After being given a picture of beautiful, colorful garden, I wrote:

This garden of beautiful greenery and flowers brings back another quaint memory of times gone by. When I left Lane Tech, as an English teacher to go south to graduate school, T, my co-worker and I visited her friend's place on the north side of Chicago.

Upon entering the bungalow, one would never imagine that as we walked towards the back and out the back door, a beautiful garden awaited. We went and sat down and the weather was mild. We sat, talked, drank wine, laughed and cried because I was about to embark on a new venture that would require that I leave old friends and trust that new ones would be forthcoming.

We were so engaged in the topics of the day that we forgot to speak of the beauty of the garden. Yet, our presence in the garden set the tone and backdrop for an unforgettable night for saying our farewells in a classic setting.

3/2009

Free write #4

After being given a picture of an outdoor library on a lawn in front of a castle, I wrote:

Can you imagine a huge bookshelf on a grassy lawn in front of a castle? What a dream! You can choose a book and stretch out and read it on the lawn or just sit cross-legged and browse.

But on first glance, I thought of the books on the Seine in Paris. Just think. There were bookstores along the waterway. What an ideal place to browse with a picturesque view along with painters working on their canvases attempting to create a replica of God's creation.

So, next to the Seine for book browsing, I would choose this green spacious lawn to choose a book or books to sit and browse on this sunny day. This is a true affirmation that writers need beauty, peace, comfort and worry-free environments to create a work of art.

(Note: I looked closer and on the picture, there was a sign on the front lawn that said Castle Bookshop.)

3/2009

Free write # 5

After being given a Popsicle stick with the word vegetable on it, I wrote:

Vegetables! I know that I should eat more of them. Wonder why most of them are green. Health is green. They help us excrete and cleanse out all of the harmful toxins and gases.

We've been told over and over by our parents, "Eat your vegetables." And, for some reason, we have always begrudged them. So, as life goes, we only find out what we need, after we've tried everything we don't need.

We buck and rail against those basic directives until we get sick and needy. Then we come back full circle and realize that Ma knew best all the time. As Robert Fulghum so simply reminded us, "All we really need to know, we learned in kindergarten." So, as for vegetables, no matter the taste or color, eat them and live, live, live.

3/2009

O Katrina!

Every time I see,
People traveling free,

Through high waters from the storm,
No longer living inside a dorm

I feel their despair and pain,
For things will never be the same.

O Katrina! You hurt so many,
Even those who once had plenty.

Now scattered across the states,
Teaching others how not to become bait.

The survivors pace on ahead,
Even though they lost their beds.

Keeping a light of hope lit,
Knowing God will restore every bit.

April 2009
Chicago, IL

(*Written after seeing pictures of the empty Lower 9th ward four years after the hurricane*)

The Day the People Stopped

He died at a golden age- 50,
On a silver date- 25,
In June –the halfway mark into the year.

He was cute as a boy
He was cute as a man,
And he even looked cute in the ambulance.

He lived in a mansion,
And was still living large
Left behind mega-music,
And is still claiming the Billboards in death!

You tell me, *'Who's Bad?'*

December 4, 2009
Chicago, IL

(Dedicated to Michael Joseph Jackson (1958- 2009)

New England Writings

Boston

There's freedom in the air, here.
I write this as I watch
 An American flag blowing in the wind.
I can breathe here.
I have breath here.
I am breathing here.

Glory be to God.
Very timely is Faith Hill's song-*Breathe*.
It's everything I thought it would be.
Cobblestone streets, trolleys, class, class
And more class.
The waterfront, sitting at Rowe's Wharf each morning-
Such an inviting sight!
Seeing all modes of transportation, airplanes
To and from Logan, water shuttles, boats, cruise boats
And of course-every morning- South Station,
Home of the almighty rail.

October 11, 2000
Boston, MA

Love Emotions

Love is a many splendored thing, yet a splendid thing.
I suppose all of those deep longings today could have been deep Yearnings
for a love I once knew.
But time either makes us forget or it makes us remember more clearly.
Some, I thought I loved were just highly favored at the time they were in
my life.
And then, there are one or two souls who will be deeply embedded within
my heart, forever.
Women, always seem to instinctively know right off the bat.
With men, they shuffle around, ducking.
Ducking, dodging doubting
And by the time they realize, that it is in fact, the *"Real McCoy*
The motion of the river has changed and it's too late.
Too late to synchronize the motion and feel the depths of the water.

3/31/2001
Boston, MA

The Saw

The day before Daddy's death date, I walked b the YWCA office and heard a bell. I instantly remembered the line from *It's a Wonderful Life* in which the little girl said "Teacher says that every time a bell rings, an angel gets its wings.'

I thought of Daddy and felt good. I said to myself," He's at peace now. He is in heaven and his good outweighed his bad." During that week, the most trying week of the year since 1979, I had a three-month interview with my boss. I mentioned Daddy and how he was always building things and how he always had us girls helping him.

My boss asked me if he was a carpenter. I said no. In my mind, I saw him sawing and me sitting on the plank acting as the balancing act. And in another conversation that week with my friend Yolanda, she mentioned how it was a good thing that he taught me independence and the ability to do things for myself.

Anyway, the day of the interview, I boarded the train and to my surprise, I looked up. There in a glass case was a saw- for emergency purposes. I stared in disbelief. The longer I stared, the more I knew that the long haul in purgatory was over! He had gotten his wings and he will always be an angel on my shoulder assisting me through this life! Praise God!

May 3, 2001
Boston, MA

Thoughts

Of course the old familiar, unsatisfying forces will try to cling,
in the wake of being shaken off.
So Shake Hard!!!

6/16/2001
Boston, MA

Love

Love is something that never really goes away,
It may subside.
Like ebb and flow or it may minimize.
And takes a backseat to priorities
But, it is always there- a *constant*.

8/12/2001
Boston, MA

A Poem for Emily

Emily,

Visiting your home evoked me to tears,
Running long and deep over pain for years.
It must have been so very hard and deep,
For you. Perils all around were so very steep.
A woman with ideas and a hefty mind.
Left in a room, world moving, but in a bind.
Watching life from a window, trudge by,
Crying, hoping. cleaving, writing with a sigh.
Heartbroken over relationships -gone astray.
And society still keeping all feelings at bay.
Kept a pen and paper close by in hand,
To stay sane while fulfilling the Master plan.
Then historians come along and try to dirty your name,
And reveal what they perceive as idiosyncratic or lame.
But I, this writer sincerely identify with you.
You had the knowledge to see rainbows and their hue.
Thank you for expressing your soul to us,
In time, all good and golden things are just!
You do wear the crown and wear it well,
Next to you, those who hurt you are all now pale.

5/2/02
Boston, MA

(Written after visiting the home of Emily Dickinson in Amherst, MA)

For You, I Am

I am.
I am the light.
I am the one you can reach out to like
A dried plant crying with all its might.

I am.
I am the sun.
I am the one, who will make you smile,
And erase the wrinkles for a mile.

I am.
I am the Truth.
I am the one, who truly loves you,
Wants you to be happy and never blue.

For I know that happiness will bring
Highest possibilities- maybe a ring.

I am.
I am comfort.
I am the one who will comfort you.
From the rough day 'til the morning dew.

You can lay your head close to my heart
The touch will give us both a new start.

For you,
I am.

May 2, 2002
Boston, MA

In Two's

All of nature travels in glorious two's
With perfect pairing, you can't lose.

Geese fly together to observe below,
Realizing the reapings they can sow.

One may fall from apparent sight,
The other rescues with all its might.

Silent communication or chattering which,
Each has an anchor to lasso or hitch.

'Tis a blessing when likes magnetically attract,
Someone special to always have your back.

5/12/02
Boston, MA

To Kay & Eddie

Life is a waterfall; always changing.
Each downpour washes anew,
As we reflect on those lives that touched ours.
When we pain over the loss,
We should be gladdened and strengthened,
By the precious memories they left behind.
Like the footprints in the sand

January 29, 2003
Boston, MA

(In memory of their friend, Jackie)

Montego Bay: A Visit

College graduation gift from parents- 1971

In 1971, we boarded a jumbo charter jet from Saturn Airlines on a trip arranged through Northeastern University in Chicago in route to Montego Bay, Jamaica. The University sponsored the trip for about 250 college students. Though we were in attendance at Chicago State University, we were allowed to go with the others.

The trip costs only $200.00 for about seven days in the sun. I remember the landing onto the island of Jamaica. Before the plane touched the ground, we were so close to the water that we could see the fish swimming in the deep blue sea. It was my first trip to the islands.

We stayed at the Chatham Beach Hotel, located right across from the beach. However, I recall doing all of my swimming in the swim pool. I remember one picture that I had where I was wearing a bikini made out of African print which my sister Cheryl had made for me.

Everyday was filled with wonderful sights and sounds of the community and its people. By us being of color, we were able to venture a little further than the other tourists. Some of the locals took us off of the tourist strip and showed us other highlights of the beautiful island.

The first ride in a car terrified us after we first left the airport. The driver drove really fast and used big horns placed on the outside of the car. The steering wheel was on the right side of the car and he drove like there was no tomorrow. I just lay down in the back seat because I was afraid to see as he went around the curves at break neck speed.

The community people called us "*souls,*" as we walked down the street. The women were often seen carrying the huge baskets of fruit or wares balanced on their heads from which they were selling items.

I remember taking a ride on a glass-bottomed boat and watching the diminishing harbor that had houses up along on high hills. In the glass bottom boat, we could see all of the creatures of the sea, which was a bit scary.

I recall the long walks and just seeing the people for themselves. Some were so poor that their houses were actually just four pieces of tin leaned together. They resided within.

And the night clubs! The art forms and the music were so real. The people were such gifted singers and dancers. Some of the dances were so amazing. The colors in the decorum were deeply rich and everything seemed to be experienced at a deeper intensity. They really knew how to turn it up a notch.

The shops were always filled with a lot of wood carvings and in some cases; the objects would catch us off guard and shock us with their sexuality. They held nothing back! And, the dining was always a nightmare, however. We could sit and wait three or four hours for a meal back then. We often ended up leaving with no meal. We would often hear, "Oh you Americans are always in a hurry." This was before fast food in the islands!

Once, we went out with some villagers who took us to the mansion of one of the high officials. The climb up and the cultured greenery were astonishing. I had a picture where I posed there at the top and on the patio of the mansion. I had on pick culottes and it was a beautifully sunny day.

They also drove us to Ocho Rios. I knew this time to just lie down in the back seat and not watch the road or the driver. This is another city on the island and is quite a distance from Montego Bay. We visited Dunn's Waterfalls. It was a delightful experience. I had a picture posing with a lot of the other students. It was so much fun. We had to climb the rocks and I witnessed nature in all of its glory.

I remember the last night we were there. I had a picture of me posing on the couch in the lobby of the Chatham Beach Hotel. It had been a wonderful experience as far as seeing how another culture lived. They were very proud of their liberation and the monuments that verified that freedom.

I ran out of money while there and called my mother for money. By the time the money order reached me, I had been home for quite some time. The letter and money order came back about two weeks after I had returned home. That is how slow and laid-back things were in Jamaica at that time.

It was so much like paradise and so tropical. It was a huge change from the hustle and bustle of the city of Chicago. I heard someone say the other day that they now have casinos there. I do not want to see that. That is why we avoided going to Kingston because we heard that it was a typical big city. I would like to remember Montego Bay just as I left it during that summer of 1971!

3/15/2003
Boston, MA

Sights and Sounds of Nassau

Trip A

I made two trips to Nassau, both in 1992. Both were done through a Fling Vacation packet. This was a package deal whereby you took a charter flight and stayed in a hotel and had a continental breakfast all for one price.

The first trip was around April of that year. I stayed at the lowest priced hotel which I believe was called the Towne Hotel. It was a blessing because it was the last stop and probably considered beneath that standards for most tourists. However, for me, it was divine. It was in the community and not on the tourist strip. I could get better acquainted with the sights and sounds of the people and get a feel of what everyday life was like there.

Interestingly enough, I was greeted and looked after by a hostess named Margarite', which is quite similar to my middle name. The hotel staff started their day about six in the morning and worked until about ten at night. Amazing, I thought. They got to know me and knew what I liked to order.

They knew that I wanted a Bahama Mama and some fritters to go. I enjoyed eating in my room after exploring the island all day. The hotel, itself, was quaint and quiet and off the beaten path. Across the street, there was an Anglican Church where all of the dignitaries went for services. I attended and took communion and heard a powerful sermon on patience, when overcoming hardships in the workplace. It was just what I needed at the time.

It was also the first time that I truly understood Christ's ascension and its place in Biblical history because the message was crystal clear. The register log had a long list of important people who had also visited this church, so I felt that I was being led to this holy place.

As I walked in the opposite direction of the church, up a hill on another day, I saw the pink government buildings. Everyday at noon, they had the changing of the guards. I did not see it, but I could see where it took place and hear them doing so from my room. I read that luminaries such as John F. Kennedy and Langston Hughes had visited there.

In the early mornings, I could hear the people up so early and working. I will always remember this sweeping of the dirt and the broken glass that could be heard as early as four in the morning. I always wondered if the man working was just keeping busy or actually doing work for which he was being paid. It remained a mystery to me

Sunday morning was beautiful. When I looked out of my window, I could see the community women and their children walking in their long colorful dresses. The girls had ribbons in their hair and it was clear that they had on their *Sunday best* and in route to the church to worship. After the service, there was an annex where they would gather and commune with one another as they enjoyed refreshments. It reminded me of my Southern roots where people really knew the meaning of Sunday and acted accordingly.

One morning, I looked out of my window and I saw a huge tail-like object. I had to know what it was. I put on my things and walked down the strip pass the shops and the Straw Market and on towards the dock called Port George. The huge tail, which I had seen from my hotel window, was the end of a cruise ship. I got as close as possible and saw passengers descending the ship. One little girl was vomiting from the sea ride. Some people were rollerblading along the side of the dock and some were standing around talking. I had never been this close to a cruise ship and it was exciting. I saw the life boats hanging from the side of the ship. I thought of the Titanic. It was a memorable sight.

After heading back towards the town, I went into the library which is in the heart of the town. It had an octagon- shape and had many pirate tales and stories in its history. I also returned to the Straw Market and visited other shops along the dock. I bought tee shirt dresses for all the women in my family and enjoyed each and every step of the way.

Later, during the trip, I joined a fellow Chicagoan that I had met on the plane. She and I met on the tourist strip at the hotel where she was staying. To me, everything there was man-made and artificial. The drinks were overly-priced but she *did* have a beach adjoined to the back of her hotel. I went and sat in one of the easy chairs and looked out over the vast blue, beautiful sea.

Just as I was about to relax and take it all in, some villagers were all upon us and trying to braid my hair and sell beads. They were asking for money. It broke the aura of paradise and gave me a feeling of sorrow for the deep poverty of the island. It really ruined my outing.

I took a bus back to my hotel and gave thanks for my quiet little affordable abode with the yellow hibiscus growing outside my window. The flowers died each night and new ones bloomed every morning

On another day, I went to a restaurant that sat right on the waterfront. It was breath-taking. The food was good and affordable. The waiters were kind and one man was *so* handsome, I had to make sure that I was not staring. As I left, I talked with one man who was so proud of his heritage and spoke of the island's freedom. As I looked over at the water, I could see young boys diving for coins that the tourists threw for them. That was painful.

When it was time to depart, I remember the airport with great detail. We had to climb the stairs to board the airplane. There were familiar faces that I had seen from the onset of the trip. They were also using the Fling package. Many of us had gone to different hotels.

We flew back to the States and landed in Savannah, Georgia. There were musicians in the airport playing island- type music. This is where each of the parties went separate ways. Some flew back to Philadelphia, New York, Los Angeles or in my case, Chicago. It was beautiful to see how our lives had touched one another's and how we then took off heading in different directions back to where we called home. I stood there waiting for my flight and recalled how great the Fling had been for me!

Trip B

The second trip was taken around August 1992. I went for a job interview for a library position. I stayed in the same hotel and recalled the fear I felt when a hurricane -like storm had doors banging in the hotel. It was something to behold.

The job did not materialize, but the people who interviewed me treated me like a long lost relative and the director invited me into his family's home. The assistant director was also very kind and showed me around the island and said the job was up to the powers that be. I appreciated her outlook on things.

Lynn M. Dixon

I also remember how the workers in the hotel looked at American television all day. They could get certain Florida channels there. This trip was more of reality check and allowed me to see what living on the island would be like. I had a friend, who had lived there for years, but I could see and fate showed me that it was not for me. I did not feel as safe the second time around but I would not take anything for the journey.

3/15/2003
Boston, MA

How? : A Short Story

"Momma? Who is my Daddy?" The child trembled.

"What?" screamed the mother. "Girl, don't start that mess today," said the mother. She advanced into a cleaning tirade. She pulled down the hanging mop, turned on the water and poured in detergent. She added some Pine-Sol and started mopping like a madwoman.

She cleaned and cleaned as though her life depended on it. As she advanced into a whirlwind, her thoughts also began to swirl. She'd have to go back through a lot of hallways and rooms to adequately answer this child's question.

But this time, the child, now 13 years old was adamant and determined to get some answers. She could see. She could see in the mirror. She could see that she did not look like anyone else in the family. She could see that her keen features and her long black hair did not match that of her siblings nor the man she called Daddy. She could see and this day, she would not be dismissed.

"How? How can I tell her? How can I tell her? the mother's inner voice anguished.

As the mother bent down to wash the baseboards, the filth and the dirt just seemed to linger. She felt like Lady Macbeth trying to wash the murdered Duncan's blood from her hands. Even if others could not see it, she could.

The voices, the memories continued to spin around in her head and loom large. As she cleaned and, she peered over at her daughter who sat there with his nose, his eyes and had his persistence.

He wouldn't leave me alone, she thought as she washed and scrubbed. He hounded me and hounded me until I broke. He was tall, dark and handsome, just like in the movies, she remembered.

"How did I know that I was the first on a long line on his list? How did I know he was picking us off? How did I know? But I can't face it. "I can't face it," she screamed.

"Face what, Momma? Me? the daughter asked.

The mother stopped cleaning and just sat on the floor and cried. The dam broke and the flood gates opened and the well of tears came forth.

She cried. She sobbed. And finally, she thought. She knew she should have told someone when he started to show up on her job everyday. She knew that he was not from that region and was intrigued by his foreign accent.

What made her think he was truly interested I her? What made her think he was sincere? Didn't she suspect that something was amiss? She was so glad to have a handsome guy from another race interested in her. Then the rendezvous came and then the unknown pregnancy. But, she thought she had it in the bag.

She went on and married her on-again and off-again boyfriend and felt that the encounter was just a memory. When her delivery date arrived, the new baby arrived, and out comes her daughter. Light? 'On well,' she thought. 'So am I'

But after three months, six months and then a year, it did not get better. Light? No, no, no. More like white, with keen features, hair reaching her waist. No wait. This wasn't supposed to happen. No. It must be a bad video. Can I edit the tape? She asked herself.

No

She waited. Her husband, a very dark man, waited. Her father waited. Her mother waited. Her sister waited. Her aunts and uncles waited. Her paternal and maternal grandparents waited. Her in-laws waited. They waited until the light became more like –white. Then they all turned into stone as horror became permanently fixated on their faces. Some cried. Some died. Some became ill. Several just fell into an eternal silence.

The ultimate disgrace! Bringing home this white-like child into a middle-class black family was truly unacceptable. She peered over to where her daughter sat and saw his face and raised her eyes toward the heavens as she prayed for the words to tell her who she was. "How?" she whispered. "How will I tell her?" And the truth began to pour from her lips as she hugged her brave daughter.

3/30/03
Boston, MA

On the Charles River

What could be more beautiful than this?
Students practicing sailing,
Kayaking
Sea gulls flying
People alive! All around
On the Charles River.
Ducks flying,
Teachers directing
Students struggling not to sink.
Couples in love.
Birds, also in couples;
A single paddler-
Retrieving dropped packets for lovers on shore,
As one male paddler did.
All on the serene and peaceful Charles River.

May 2003
Boston, MA

Ode to My Mother

There are no words, when a mother's gone.
O silence, before all nations!
Lament, sorrow, grief abound,
Dark hours seem to stay and plague.
Sorrow seems to envelop the soul
And death leaves its cold sting.
Tears and then years of reflection surface,
Corners turned and conversations held.

August 2003
Boston, MA

He: A Short Story

"He's more that a woman can take!" she blurted out.

"He's a sad, sad, sad man and with each breath he takes, he draws three breaths of life from others."

People standing around the bar ordering drinks looked over at her and voices lowered. The waitress in the tiny bar was running late so people had to go to the bar and order their own drinks before proceeding to a table. So, she, the speaker, sat on the bar stool, swirled around towards her audience and began to spin her yarn.

"I knew he wore a wedding band but he did not act married. He flirted as though it had no real meaning, so what's a single girl to think?" she continued.

The bartender kept pouring drinks, filling requests as quickly as he could. She poured out her story and the light over her seat seemed to glow over her head as a spotlight. The band had not arrived, so here sat the present entertainment.

"So we started seeing each other. He told me he was divorcing his wife and was in litigation. I believed him," she went on.

She paused for a sip from her Bloody Mary. Two women, who were tourists, looked at each other. One said, "That sounds like what happened to my sister." They got their drinks and continued to talk as they found a table.

"Next thing I know," the wife was outside my apartment looking for me. She wanted to see who I was and wanted to know if I was carrying her husband's child."

People tried to ignore the speaker but one of the two guys receiving drinks said, "Man doesn't that should like Charlie's case?'

"Yes," replied his friend as they moved toward a table, still talking about Charlie.

"Anyway," she went on, "I told her that I was only *seeing* her husband and if there was a baby coming, I wasn't carrying it because it takes more than seeing to make a baby." She paused again and took another sip of her Bloody Mary. She drew in a deep breath and continued spinning.

"As if that wasn't enough, he was really seeing my close friend. They were making me look like the heavy and using me as the scapegoat. She really was pregnant with his child. Children can't stay secret for long, as you all know. The wife was warm, but just on the wrong track," she puttered.

Two *best* friends were still waiting in line for their drinks. One started fidgeting and said to the other," Could you order me a pina colada? I need to go the ladies room and I'll go find us a table," she scurried away in a half jog. This story was hitting too close to home.

"And," the now entertainer said," He was in contact with my brother. Told him how much he loved me but was afraid of my rejection so he had my brother telling him all about me and keeping up with my moves so he could use me as the fall guy in his many antics."

The last two guys in line looked at each other. One said, "Man, I could never do that to my sister. Nobody better not ask me nothing about my sister," he state emphatically. "I know," said his partner. "It reminds me of …." And these voices continued in a low murmur as they walked in the direction of an empty table.

The spotlight over the woman seemed to dim. The waitress showed up looking apologetic and disheveled. The band had arrived and started its first set with "Lost in Love." The woman finished her drink, looked around at all of the group therapy sessions going on at each table all set in motion from the tale she had spun.. She eased off the stool, left the bar and smiled as she walked out into the brisk night air.

7/22/2003
Boston, MA

If You Only Have a Day in Boston
(Written as travel magazine submission)

If you only have a day in Boston and you do not want to take a guided tour, here's a walking tour of some of Boston's highlights concentrating on the Back Bay area. You will need bounds of energy, good walking shoes and about three and four hours.

Start your tour of South Station. Come out at the exit on Summer Street and head east and turn left on Dorchester Avenue. Walk one block and on the waterfront, you will see the Boston Tea Ship & Museum and the Children's Museum is across the waterfront. The ship will reopen in 2004, due to a fire in 2001.

Reverse your steps and return to the front of South Station, but this time head west on Summer Street and go pass it. Walk about four blocks until you see the historic Macy's to your left and Filene's Basement on your right. You have just entered Boston's Downtown Crossing. Explore. There is an inexpensive eatery there on the northeast corner called the Corner Mall. Just remember to watch the clock. There is so much more to see.

Get back on Summer Street, which may have changed names to Winter Street on you, but keep heading west to the end of the street. Cross the street (Tremont) and you have entered the famous Boston Commons. So much history has taken place here, so do your homework. If you look up, you will see the gold-domed State House. That is Beacon Hill where legislature takes place.

Make a left turn towards the middle of Boston Commons and head south. You will see a lot of statues, interesting people and perhaps a protest, a Shakespearean play or even ice skating, depending on the time of year. But keep heading south until you arrive at Charles Street.

Cross the street and you have entered Boston's Public Gardens. You will probably be taken with all of the wonderful statues and of course, the Swan boats, if in season. Take a few minutes and take a ride if time and weather permits. It is a short and sweet ride.

When you are exiting the public Gardens at Arlington Street, you should try to come out at the beautiful statue of George Washington riding on a horse. If you see birds perched on his shoulder or his hat, don 't think that they are a part of the monument and don't be surprised when they start flying away after sitting still for so long and fooling the spectators.

If you look to the left, you sill see the Ritz-Carleton and if you look straight ahead, you will have a one-point perspective of the Commonwealth Mall. It is the Parisian-styled Commonwealth Avenue with statues erected all down the middle grove of the avenue. The first statue you will see is the honorable Alexander Hamilton draped in his sheath before his duel. There are others including abolitionist William Lloyd Garrison down the way, but at this point, you should turn right and head westward and enter the Arthur Fielder footbridge. Cross over and you will see the Hatch Shell where musical concerts take place and of course straight is the Charles River.

Get as close to the famed Charles River as you like, but head south so can you enjoy the sailboats, kayaking or whatever water activities are taking place. But keep a check on your watch. You know when you want to be back to your hotel.

When you get to the next footbridge, crossing back over the expressway, turn left and cross it heading east and walk back four blocks. You should be traveling east on Dartmouth and once you cross Commonwealth Avenue and go one block, you should make a right turn heading south on the shoppers paradise, Newbury Street. Head south, shop and enjoy!

When you get to Gloucester, the streets are alphabetically named, make a left turn or head east. One block over you are now on Boston's main street called Boylston. You will see the huge Hynes Convention Center straight ahead but you will want to cross over and go about a half of a block north. There you will want to enter the Prudential Shops. It is a gala affair so pick up a brochure inside at the information booth. Just ask. And, if you see a large picturesque white porcelain- line dome, sitting to your south from inside the Prudential, that is the Mother Church, the home church of the Christian Scientists.

The shops in the Prudential stretch all the way across Huntington Avenue and there are some great restaurants. Ask about all of the attractions including the Top View of the Hub. You are almost finished with the inexpensive way to see some of Boston's main sights.

When you exit the Prudential Shops and head north on Boylston Street, be sure to walk at least back up to Dartmouth Street which about two blocks. You will see the country's oldest public library, The Boston Public Library sitting to your right. If time permits, tours are given inside this historic landmark.

And last, but not least you will see the famed Copley Square where many art shows, farmers' market, ice shows, concerts or some bazaars are held, again depending on the time of year. Trinity Church is located to the north of the square and it also offers tours. If time permits, go inside and see the old Puritan-styled pulpit that sits high above the congregation.

Okay. Whew. You are now tired, so why not take a cab back to your hotel? Look at your watch and see how you have done since you only had one day in Boston. Relax and cherish the memories of the illustrious Boston walking tour.

7/23/2003
Boston, MA

Thirteen Bread Days in December:
A Children's story

Stanley woke up to the smell of coffee from his Grandmother's kitchen. He felt safe here. He looked around and heard the ticking of his father's clock.

"Better get up," he thought.

No noise. Just peace. No loud music and people coming and going like at his mother's house. He was glad to be living here. As the smells from the kitchen entered his nostrils, Stanley thought, "It's thinking time." That is what his grandmother called the quiet mornings. Thinking time.

So that is what he started doing. He wiped his eyes and got up and let his feet touch the warm rug by his bed. He went to the bathroom and washed and brushed his teeth and started thinking about his school project. His mind slowed when he remembered that it was Saturday. He breathed.

"Thirteen? What will he do with the number 13? "he wondered. His teacher had given him that number and he had to come up with a creative way to use it for a Christmas project.

After he was all clean and in clean weekend clothes, he joined his grandmother in the kitchen. "Hi, baby," she said.

"Good morning, Grandma," he answered.

"Today, I will be doing a lot of baking for the church, so I might need you to run some errands."

"Okay," replied Stanley. "What are you baking?"

"Bread. Loaves and loaves of bread," she said.

So, Stanley thought and thought. "Everybody needs bread," he thought.

He then told her about his school project and how bread could be his answer.

"I could give out thirteen loaves of bread in the community. I will think of places that could use them," he said.

After he ate his eggs, hash browns, sausage and toast, he felt full and full of ideas. He helped wash the dishes as he had been taught. He took out the trash and when he turned towards his Grandma, she said, "I have an idea. I will pay you for the errands that you run for me and you can buy your 13 loaves of bread. We cannot give out my baked bread because everyone would not feel comfortable with homemade bread," she added.

Stanley, now in the fifth grade, went to his room and started writing down ideas at his desk. He always kept paper and pen close by to capture fresh ideas as they flowed. He had seen how his grandmother always made lists of things to do or grocery lists. He had learned from observing and he saw that she usually had a plan and scratched off the things after they had been completed.

So, he started his list with grandmother's help and wrote down the 13 places in the community that he would deliver a loaf of bread. Most of these places had a bin for Christmas donations. He listed: the local library, the post office, the church, the fire station, the police station, the Yates family of nine, the homeless shelter, the town hall, the park district, the newspaper office and the local department store. He had eleven places.

He paused. He put down his pen and went on the back porch to walk away from the list and think. He peered into the sky as if looking for more answers. He felt someone's presence and saw his friend Robert. He told him about his project and told him that he needed two more places to add to his list to have 13 places to deliver a loaf of bread.

"I know," said Robert. What about the place with the golden top? "

"Oh, you mean the State House. We learned about it in social studies. Okay. That is a good idea!" replied Stanley.

"And, what about the lady with the cart?" added Robert.

"Perfect," said Stanley.

He then asked Robert if he would go with him to deliver a loaf a day and help him find the food box, as his Grandmother had called it. Robert, two years older than Stanley, said he would be glad to go with him to deliver after he asked his mother. Stanley thanked him and went back inside to add the last two things to his list. He took off his thinking cap

95

and spent the rest of the day running errands for his granny and playing as he threw a few balls with Robert. Every time he made some money for going to the store, he put it in his cigar box which was his bank.

He went to the store three times, ran the vacuum, dried the dishes as his granny cooked and made sure that his bed was made and all his gadgets in his room were in their proper places. He had learned a lot about neatness and order since he had been living with his granny. He felt better about every thing when he could put his hands on things.

So, on Monday, he turned in his project title to his teacher and called it *Thirteen Bread Days in December.* He wrote a paragraph explaining his plan of action and his teacher beamed and told him how creative he was. After school, he and Robert went to their first place of delivery together. Both his granny and Robert's mother felt safer with them going to these places as a team and anxiously watched the clock every day until they were home.

Before he and Robert went into the library, Stanley listened to the sounds of Christmas in the air. He heard people singing, music playing and the bells ringing while people asked for help for the needy. The community was truly in the spirit.

He loved the local library with all of the books from which to choose. When they entered, he asked where the food drop box was and the guard in a dark blue uniform smiled and pointed to a corner where he saw a crate labeled Food Drop Box. He placed his first loaf of bread in the box.

He noticed the woman sitting behind the desk operating a scanning machine and a line of people waiting with loads of books in their arms. He smiled as he left through the rotating doors and their parents smiled when they returned home. After dinner, Stanley went into his room and entered his observations from the library visit into his journal. He was getting a chance to see how different people made a living and he was taking it all in.

On day two, he and Robert went in the post office. He remembered to look for a large American flag which is something else he had learned in his social studies class. Once inside, he noticed that the men and women had on white shirts and blouses and dark pants. Again, they were in uniforms. There were long lines of people with large and small packages, trying to get packages to certain places by Christmas, as Robert explained. They found the drop box, dropped the loaf of bread, left and went out into the blustery day.

On day three, they went to the local church. He and Robert laughed and joked along the way everyday and it made the assignment seem more like an exciting adventure. In the church, the big lady with the big, beautiful voice that serenaded the congregation on Sundays was glad to help them and show them where to drop the donated loaf of bread.

Day four found them entering the local fire station. Stanley studied the huge red fire truck with its hoses and equipment. He saw how the firemen sat around talking and playing a game of cards as they relaxed until they were needed to battle a fire. They had on undershirts, visible suspenders and rubber boots. He had read how dangerous this type of work could be for the firemen. They were very friendly towards him and Robert and pointed towards the donation box. At night, Stanley made entries into his journal as his excitement heightened.

The police station was easy to find on the fifth day of delivery. The cars with the lights on top and the activity all around made the station easy to recognize. He noted the dark uniforms with the star badges that the men and women wore. There was little laughter and he knew from looking at the nightly news that law enforcement was no laughing matter. He felt a little fear and a lot of respect. A nice female officer pointed to the donation box after he nervously told her why they were there. They left without hesitation and were relieved when the air hit their faces on that day.

Day six was simple. Robert said, "You can do this one by yourself." He went down the block and rang the Yates family bell. He waited and asked for Mrs. Yates. He explained his school project and asked if she would help him by allowing him give her family a loaf of bread. She paused and then smiled and said," I would be honored to accept the loaf of bread." As he walked down the steps from her porch, he breathed a sigh of relief and shook Robert's hand when he met him at the corner.

Robert and Stanley saw the men hanging around the front of the next establishment. They were smoking and seemed to be cracking jokes while some were selling a paper called *Streetwise*. This was the homeless shelter and this was their seventh day. He and Robert were very quiet as they witnessed these men who seemed to be down on their luck. Yet, he saw a certain joy and they asked them their names. They explained why they were there and two of the men pointed them towards the main office. As they turned to leave, the men said, "Bye Robert and Stanley and Merry Christmas!" Stanley wrote about the men and how he would always remember the laughter these men enjoyed in spite of their circumstances.

At the local town hall, day eight, he saw men in business suits and women dressed very expensively. They pointed to the donation box out to them and Stanley was so impressed with their clothes. He later talked to his grandmother about it and she talked to him about the importance of education if he thought he wanted a job wearing nice business suits one day. She also talked about the importance of their work and how the decisions they made could affect all of the people in the neighborhood. He had a lot to write that night.

Day nine was fun. Stanley and Robert went to the park district office. There were a lot of children playing all types of activities in afterschool programs. The coaches all had on the same color tee shirts and had whistles hanging around their necks. After they dropped off the loaf of bread, they were allowed to bounce a few basketballs.

The next day, they went into the local newspaper office which was their tenth day. Stanley noted the large glass window with a group of men and women typing on their laptops. The atmosphere was tense and Stanley later learned about the deadlines that they were trying to meet in order put out a paper. One man looked up, pointed to the donation box and signaled for them to take a free newspaper. His granny helped explain what they do at the newspaper. She also told him how they must now compete with the Internet. He wrote that night in his journal and talked about how much his granny knew and how much she read and shared things with him.

Going to the department store was a breeze for Stanley and Robert. Who wouldn't enjoy a store at Christmas time? He saw the nice ties and smelled the nice men's fragrances as he took the escalator up to Customer Service to make his donation on day eleven. A nice lady gave them a big thank you and called them by their names. Their good work had been the talk of the community and people were expecting them. Robert and Stanley felt a great sense of pride on that day at the department store.

On day twelve, Stanley's grandmother surprised him and said, "Today, I am going with you. Robert can come along if he wants. I want to see the State House for myself. So they took the train this time and the three of them climbed the hill and entered the building with the gold dome. The building was even more beautiful on the inside and had a lot of portraits of great lawmakers on the walls. The man at the front desk was also in uniform and seemed to be retirement age. He was pleasant and showed them where the donation box was located. His granny said as they descended the steps, "Thank you Stanley for giving me this opportunity.

I always wanted to go in there but never had a reason before now," she smiled.

When he wrote in his journal, he wrote about the lawmakers that he had seen. They had on suits and carried briefcases and seemed to walk fast as if they had somewhere to go and something important to do. He saw organization and order in action.

Day thirteen was the last day. He decided to do this one alone. He had his loaf of bread wrapped specially and went out looking for the lady with the cart on the corner. As he turned the corner, he looked for her. She was not there and his heart dropped. He felt a bit of sadness and wondered if she was okay. This had to be a hard life for her and they assumed that she would always be there. He started home slowly. And then, he heard some creaky wheels. He turned and there she was! He told her about his project and held out the wrapped loaf of bread. She smiled a toothless smile and said, "God bless you, child." She hugged him and he returned the hug around her waist. They parted and he went home feeling tired, relieved, happy and fulfilled inside. His mission was accomplished.

When he was in his room, he had a lot of thoughts to add to his journal. He wrote and wrote and the words just kept on coming. Afterwards, he got on his knees and said a special prayer for the woman with the cart. He prayed that she had a nice warm bed to sleep in as he did every night.

He had seen so much during those thirteen days of delivering loaves of bread. As he stilled his thoughts, he thought of all of the possibilities. He had so many types of jobs to choose from and he has seen so many things that take place right there in the community. As he fell asleep, that night, he dreamed of himself in some of those suits and uniforms. His choices were endless.

6/21/2004
Boston, MA